MYTH QUEST
Jatayu

SAVIOUR FROM THE SKIES

retold by Anu Kumar

illustrations by Maya Magical Studios

First published in 2011 by Hachette India
An Hachette UK company

www.hachetteindia.com

10 9 8 7 6 5 4 3 2

ISBN: 978-93-5009-284-2

Hachette India
612/614 (6th Floor), Time Tower
MG Road, Sector 28, Gurgaon 122001, India

Typeset in Adobe Garamond Pro 13/16 by
Eleven Arts, New Delhi

Printed in India by
Manipal Press Ltd, Manipal

Welcome to the world of MythQuest…

Discover the fables and legends about the origin, history, deities, ancestors and heroes of India.

While the term 'myth' in common conversation means a false story, in the world of religion, folklore and magic, myths are considered 'true'. They tell stories of the creation of the universe, the eternal battle between good and evil, and the history of humankind itself.

The main characters in our myths are bigger and better than any modern superheroes. They are birds and beasts, gods and demons, kings and queens, generals and warriors, sages and gurus, each with extraordinary powers that changed the course of history and the fate of the human race.

The people to whom a myth belongs consider it a true account of their past millions of years ago. Even today, they continue to worship the gods and goddesses, follow the rituals and read the texts that developed from these myths.

Hachette's MythQuest series brings to you fascinating stories from the vast treasures of ancient mythology. Read them all—and become a MythMaster!

Mythological characters and events have been described in different ways in different versions of ancient texts. We have chosen the most interesting and key stories to build a comprehensive account for the young reader.

This book is about . . .

. . . Jatayu, a vulture of the deva *or celestial dynasty, and the king of vultures. This great bird has been mentioned in the Ramayana, the Mahabharata as well as Puranic texts. He is generally understood to be the grandson of the sage Kashyapa and Vinata, who in turn was the daughter of Daksha Prajapati, one of Lord Brahma's thousand sons. Jatayu's father was Aruna and his mother was Grdhri, a bird. Jatayu's mother was the daughter of Tamra, the mother of vultures, curlews and all birds. That's why Jatayu is also called the king of birds.*

Jatayu was well endowed with the wisdom of sages and knowledge of dharma*—the rules that laid down what was right and what was wrong. He had an extraordinary wingspan, making him appear like an immense mountain in flight, if you can imagine such an unusual sight. Artists over the ages have often drawn Jatayu as a Himalayan griffon vulture.*

In one place in the texts, Jatayu refers to himself as sixty thousand years old, so we do know he lived for many, many years, and was quite, quite old. He is held up as a symbol of courage, true friendship and exemplary loyalty.

Here is Jatayu's story, full of highs and lows . . .

CHAPTER ONE

TWO BROTHERS IN THE SKIES

It was a time when the birds had their kingdom deep in a forest, a secret place that very few knew about. Perhaps the gods did, but not many human beings had been there. It was a retreat close to the river Godavari, green with trees, and lush with plenty of fruits and tubers. It was called Panchavati and this was where the king of the birds lived.

Somewhere in the middle of this forest, on a rocky plateau, sat Jatayu, the most magnificent of bird-kings. He was as massive as a mountain, with wings as widespread as a rain-cloud, and swift as the wind, with the proud and matchless lustre of golden sunlight, and able to cover long distances without a sign of exhaustion. His eyes, just as that of his brother Sampati, were wise and sharp and keen, and able to see as far as 20 *yojanas*—a distance of nearly two thousand full-grown elephants standing end to end.

Jatayu was older than most things on earth, older than the trees most definitely, older even than the mountains. But of course, there was someone else who was older than he was, and that was his elder brother, Sampati.

Sampati, meanwhile, observed the world from his perch on the mountain Mahendra Parvat, where he lived under the protection of sage Nishakara, who was performing a penance there. Besides being hard to reach, Mahendra Parvat was also one of the most sacred places on earth.

The birds knew that as long as Sampati and his brother, Jatayu, managed their affairs, things would be all right. Their world would run the way it was supposed to—seasons would change, trees would flower in spring and wither in winter, and the birds would migrate, move north and south with the Sun God, raise families, and carry out the daily rituals of their lives peacefully.

But no one can predict when things can change suddenly and when one's luck can run out.

And who knew this better than the two brothers! For once upon a time, Sampati had been able to spread his

majestic wings out in the sky, and they had gleamed and glinted as they caught the sunlight. Sampati's speed and alacrity had been all too well known.

Now he was flightless, unable to span the skies as he had once in his youth.

CHAPTER TWO

THE RACE TO THE SUN

Their names were always taken together, in the same breath . . . Sampati and Jatayu. The two brothers had always been inseparable. They were the sons of Grdhri and Aruna, who was the Sun God Surya's loyal charioteer. Their uncle—Aruna's brother, Garuda—was a divine bird and Lord Vishnu's chosen mount. He was someone both Sampati and Jatayu looked up to. Garuda ferried Lord Vishnu around to most places, for as the Preserver of the Universe, Lord Vishnu had a lot of business to attend to. He usually rested on the serpent Adishesha, and when he arose, Garuda would carry him at a speed faster than anyone could ever imagine. Garuda was strong and huge, and sometimes when he flew at great heights, he could even block the path of Surya, giving his brother Aruna some anxious moments as he drove the Sun God in his chariot on his daily journey across the sky.

Aruna watched over his sons Sampati and Jatayu as they often raced high in the sky to reach him. That would irritate Surya, so Aruna asked Sampati, the older of the two brothers, to keep an eye on Jatayu. The young birds were very adventurous and Aruna was always worried about them.

'Be careful flying around like that, high in the sky,' Aruna would warn his young ones. 'Don't come too close, ever.' But like all young ones, they would not always listen. He was proud of them all the same as they made such a fine spectacle flying across the skies, covering vast distances in a trice. The flapping of their wings was like the whirring of leaves on a giant tree. In the wake of their flight, the winds sent clouds rushing out of the way, setting up storms, small and strong. And their mighty wings would cast dark shadows upon the earth.

However, for all his caution, there was little Aruna could have done on the day of the great race between Sampati and Jatayu.

Aruna did not know whose idea it was, but suddenly as he was guiding Surya's chariot in the sky, his view was blocked. He could barely make out anything. And then he saw the familiar silhouettes of his two sons as they flew determinedly right up to where he was navigating the chariot of the Sun God.

It was summer, and Surya was at his most splendid, and fiercest, staring unblinkingly down on earth, leaving a blazing trail of heat and light. Surya had left it to Aruna to steer his fine white horses in the right direction, and Aruna efficiently followed a set path every day.

Aruna gesticulated wildly, cautioning the two birds away from the fiery Surya. But they kept coming, unheedingly, their wings cresting and falling like gigantic waves in the sky. The two young birds flew higher and higher. The span of their wings filled up the vast blue expanse, dimming in many places the harsh glare of the summer sun. The shadow their wings cast swept across the earth, covering mountains, lakes, rivers, fields, villages and towns. The shadows moved as the two brothers did, racing each other madly, crazily, hoping to reach Surya before the other did.

Jatayu was younger, but he was stronger and swifter. It was a neck-and-neck race, as Sampati and he flew over the highest mountains and through dense clouds. They felt the air around them thin and the heat start to singe their backs. Their breathing grew harsher and more ragged, but they were not going to give up.

When they were high up, very high, all that could be heard was the beating of their wings—it was a noise louder than the roar of the oceans and the shaking of a thousand trees in the forest, more terrifying than the march of a hundred elephants on the move.

They were flying so high that neither realized how close he was getting to the sun. They thought it was just tiredness that was making them feel

hot and breathless. So close were they to the Sun God by then that the simmering, sizzling heat made their eyes glaze.

Then Sampati felt a strong blast of heat on his large beak, on his hooded forehead, on his magnificent multicoloured plumage. He heard the stamping of horses . . . and he knew they were in certain and grave danger.

CHAPTER THREE

FOR THE PRICE OF WINGS

Sampati heard the pounding of the Sun God's chariot. He knew that Surya's chariot was unstoppable, that his father could not pause, that the universe and everything in it was clocked by the Sun God completing his journey on time.

He saw his brother Jatayu now burst ahead in a new surge of speed. Sampati knew his brother had still not understood the danger that lay ahead. If Jatayu got any closer, he would surely be burnt alive. Surya never really cared for anything that stood in his path, always blazing relentlessly ahead in his unchanging movement across the skies.

Bracing himself against the heat, catching his breath for an infinitesimal moment, Sampati spread his wings as wide as they would stretch. He then breathed in the hot air in huge gulps and prepared to make the most important flight of his life. He had to catch up with his brother Jatayu—and save him.

Jatayu, meanwhile, was so keen on winning against Sampati in the race that he was oblivious to what could happen. He rushed ahead, heedless of what lay before him. Or above him.

And above him, his wings bristling with a sense of imminent disaster, flew Sampati, hurrying ahead, closer and closer to the Sun God. The heat scorched his skin, left burning whiplashes wherever it could find vulnerable, exposed skin.

As Sampati looked down below, he saw Jatayu race on towards him, and he desperately spread his wings even wider, not flinching as the searing heat clung to him like a spreading forest fire. He stretched, his unmoving wings spread out like a colossal dark cloud over his brother.

He stood there, unwavering like a rock in the empty blue sky, not wincing as the heat tore into him. He bit back screams of pain as his fine feathers caught fire. He could hear the flames crackle, as they spread

in a fury, tearing up his luxuriant plumage. The black and white tail feathers, the golden softer ones on his back, and the sleeker white feathers that underlay these, were soon alight in orange flares of fire. Still Sampati stayed there, his eyes fixed unblinkingly on his younger brother.

It was only a long time later, when he could no longer bear the pain, when his fine feathers were charred black, and his wings hung limply by his side, that Sampati tumbled down, in pain and sorrow, unable to spread his once magnificent wings.

He fell, with all his strength now gone, his useless wings like broken wands on either side, dropping feathers as thick as small black clouds as he plummeted and fell, flightless, to the earth.

His father Aruna drove straight ahead, tears clouding his vision. Jatayu, shocked beyond words, could say little, his voice coming out in croaks and his guilty tears flowing unabated.

Aruna, moved by his son's great sacrifice to save the brother he so loved, blessed him, 'You are truly your brother's keeper, my son. But your sacrifice will not go in vain. One day, your wings will be restored when a divine soul who truly understands the meaning of brotherly devotion and loyalty comes by.'

Sampati had saved his brother unhesitatingly, but his wings were useless now and he could no longer rule over the birds. From being a magnificent, powerful bird that could fly anywhere and everywhere, he was now weakened and disabled. The elders in his clan, all the other wise birds, and the gods who decided such things, made up their minds that it would be Jatayu who would be the king of birds instead. Still every bird respected

Sampati's wisdom and foresight, and everyone had been moved by what he had done.

'My son,' said Aruna, 'the mountain called Mahendra Parvat is where you shall live now. From there you shall keep an eye on everything.' Then with a knowing nod cast Jatayu's way, Aruna added, 'Especially the things your brother could get up to.'

Mahendra Parvat was one of the most difficult places to reach on earth. Its abundance of flowering plants and fruit trees and many animals was legendary. This was where the sage Parashurama, known for his fierce temper, would sleep every night. This is where Sampati spent his days, under the kind and protective eye of the sage Nishakara.

CHAPTER FOUR

AN ARROW AND A FRIENDSHIP

Jatayu lived in Panchavati for a great many years, watching over with wisdom and compassion all matters of the forest and the affairs of birds.

One day, as he roamed the skies, his sharp eyes saw a hunting party on the move. He saw that the group of hunters was led by Dasharatha, the mighty king of Ayodhya. He had distinguished himself in battle against Ravana, the demon king of Lanka. Dasharatha and Ravana nursed an old and continuing enmity since the time Ravana had had the cheek to ask Dasharatha for a tribute, something that could be demanded of only a lesser vassal.

Dasharatha's response had been to angrily dismiss the messenger Ravana had sent all the way from his kingdom in the south. Then taking aim, for Dasharatha was still very angry, he had let loose a volley of arrows in the direction of Lanka. The arrows he had aimed shot up straight into the sky, sending fiery sparks in every direction, before they zoomed off with certainty towards the south, where Lanka was. Dasharatha was the finest archer of his time, and would always be held up for later archers as the one to emulate.

The arrows he shot found their mark, as Dasharatha had never missed before and wouldn't then. They flew faster than light, noiseless and silent through the air, covering the distance to Lanka in a flash. When Ravana returned to his capital from a hunt, he found his entry barred, for the arrows had sealed the city gates in a very effective manner. This was very humiliating for Ravana, who considered himself the greatest and most powerful of kings. When he was prevented from

entering his own capital because of the arrows blocking the entrance, he swore to wreak revenge.

Jatayu had heard the story, of course, and now he watched as Dasharatha wandered off from the rest of his group. It was a thick forest and one could easily lose one's way in its many entangled shrubs, vines and leafy bushes. Jatayu kept track of the king, and his sharp eyes could spot him clearly even where the forest was at its thickest, with trees packed so close together that even light could not pass.

But an arrow did.

As he moved his head, following Dasharatha's every move, an arrow whistled past Jatayu's head. It landed on a rock not too far away, and he saw a fox run away from its hiding place, and a flock of birds fluttered up, panicked, in the air. And soon after, followed by the tramping of feet, and the rustling of leaves, there emerged Dasharatha himself, looking equally surprised at seeing Jatayu.

'You missed, King of Ayodhya,' Jatayu said, looking at the king from under his hooded eyes.

Dasharatha looked most displeased with himself. His armlets of gold and his armour of metal glinted, and taking off his crown, he shook his hair loose. 'You looked like an *asura* sitting there on those rocks. And it's rare that I miss.'

'Well, this is one occasion on which you did miss,' said Jatayu in his low, gravelly voice, 'I heard the twang of your bow as you released the arrow, and heard it whistle as it moved through air.'

These words were the beginning of a firm friendship between the king of birds, Jatayu, and the great king of Ayodhya, Dasharatha.

'I am lost,' admitted the king finally, as he stood on the rocky plateau and looked down at the forest all around him. A vast sea of green surrounded them, and Dasharatha looked so bewildered that Jatayu decided to help him.

'I can see my way through these forests easily. You just need to follow me as I fly overhead. And remember,

should you ever need help, you have only to shoot arrows in the sky, and I will rush to your aid.'

Then Jatayu escorted Dasharatha through the forest. Soon, they were at the frontier of the jungle, and the path to Ayodhya stretched open and clear. The king's soldiers and men were most relieved, and there were shouts of joy at seeing Dasharatha back safe and sound. Jatayu rested on a tree impassively as the royal procession passed below him, and the king looked back in farewell.

Neither of them knew that he would come to the other's aid sooner than expected.

CHAPTER FIVE

BATTLES IN THE SKIES

Now King Dasharatha had four sons, and he was very proud of all of them. Rama was the eldest, the ideal crown prince. Once he came of age, he married Sita, daughter of King Janaka of Mithila, in a *swayamvara*, a ceremony where she chose him as her husband from among many princes. Sita's younger sister was married to Rama's younger brother Lakshmana, while Rama's other two brothers, Bharata and Shatrughana, married Sita's cousins.

Everyone returned home to great festivities and celebrations that lasted for days. Each house wore a new look, there were flower decorations in courtyards, and the palace of King Dasharatha was the most lavishly done up of all, of course.

The marriage of Rama and Sita was a blissful one. The two kingdoms of Mithila and Ayodhya were the most powerful in the land, and their joining hands meant that no one could dare challenge them.

Unfortunately, only a few months later, the rains failed. The summer that year was hotter than anyone remembered. The hot winds blew from the west and dried up everything. Crops yellowed and withered, fields developed cracks that deepened as the Sun God blazed down mercilessly, with little respite. Queues of people began appearing before the palace, pleading to the king for mercy.

'Give us food,' they begged. 'All our crops are shrivelling up in the fields.'

Dasharatha was already troubled. Once, while hunting, he had mistaken the bubbling sound of a pitcher being filled at the river Sarayu for the sound of a boar and shot an arrow that had accidentally killed a young man called Shravana Kumar. The youth had been a dutiful son, who had left his sightless parents by the river bank, to fetch them water. Dasharatha's arrow had killed him instantly, and Shravana's distraught father had cursed Dasharatha that he too would be separated from his son and die of the grief it would cause him.

Now sitting on his throne, seeing misery everywhere, Dasharatha wanted to ensure that nothing disturbed his kingdom further. He threw open the doors of the royal granaries, ordered the building of more canals and consulted all the religious men of his kingdom, for Dasharatha was very particular about rituals and wanted to do everything right. They shook their heads, and looked very serious until a very nervous Dasharatha had to ask them what the matter was.

The religious experts studied the situation and said, 'Sir, it's Lord Shani who is the culprit. It is his evil eye that is responsible for all the hard times the people in your kingdom are suffering. You must go up to him and plead. There is no other way to reach him.'

Now Shani was a *deva*, the son of Surya and his wife Chhaya, and one god everyone liked to steer clear of. Brahma, the Creator of the Universe, had extracted a promise from Shani, that he would not cast his evil eye on anyone—for a simple glance from Shani could consign a person to flames in no time. So Dasharatha was taking a big risk in going up to Shani to challenge him.

Dasharatha rode into the skies in his chariot. Shani didn't want a confrontation; he knew Dasharatha was armed with a weapon he had been given by the gods, and he had to heed his promise to Brahma as well. He had no intention of taking on Dasharatha's ire, and from behind the clouds, he saw the king make swift progress, covering the miles in no time.

The chariot Dasharatha rode himself, made its way swiftly through the clouds. Sometimes he shot arrows to clear particularly heavy clouds or divert a comet or

two. Higher and higher Dasharatha's chariot went, the horses tearing through the sky.

Meanwhile, Jatayu was following Dasharatha's every move as he made his determined way to Shani. He flexed his wings and began to fly up to be of help to the king once he reached Shani.

Meanwhile, Shani, his eyes half closed, watched Dasharatha approach. Remembering the promise he had made to Brahma, he dared not turn and catch Dasharatha's eyes. As he felt him come closer, ever closer, Shani's eyes opened wider, and flames of fire flickered into shape. The corners of the clouds were soon afire.

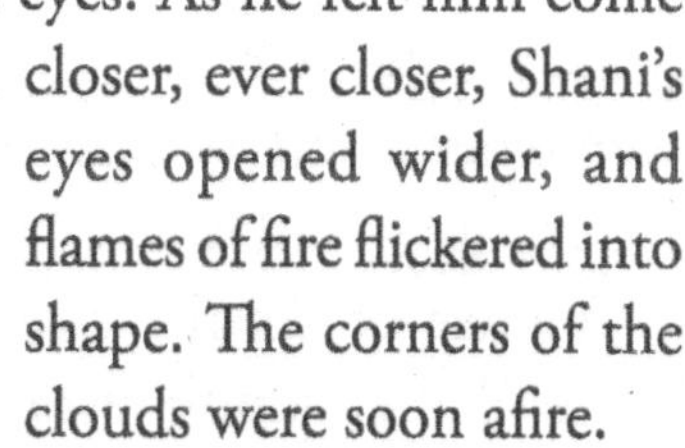

Shani knew that if Dasharatha caught up with him, and he happened to look directly at the king, the gods would punish him for breaking his promise. There was Jatayu too, following in Dasharatha's wake. He could hear the flapping of Jatayu's mammoth wings and knew that in no time the bird would also soon be at his side. He had heard of Jatayu's race to reach the Sun God, and how his brother Sampati had protected him.

Shani could move fast if he wanted to. He was agile—with legs and arms that could stretch in several directions at once. And he was on wings too, that of his mount—a raven, yet he was finding it hard to evade Dasharatha and Jatayu.

Below, not too far behind, Jatayu could see Dasharatha. Then an arrow brushed past his feet, and Jatayu took a swipe at Shani with his large beak. Shani could see the bird-king's yellow beady eyes and feel the pain where Jatayu's beak had slashed at him.

The great bird opened his mouth in a snarl.

A gust of smoke and fire burst out of Shani's lips and the clouds were swept aside. He could feel the pinpricks of pain as Dasharatha's arrows struck him everywhere.

The bird was very close. The rush of steaming air that swirled around him as Jatayu came up faster and faster threatened to engulf Shani. He was tiring. It had been a mad rush across the universe, passing planets and stars, skirting asteroids and meteorites following their own random paths, and Dasharatha and Jatayu were still close on his heels.

Still, Shani wasn't giving up without a fight. He cast a last baleful glance at Dasharatha's chariot not far behind and at once it caught fire. Flames erupted and sent sparks shooting in all directions from the wheels of the chariot. Soon, Dasharatha too heard the crackle of wood, felt the spitting of fire at his feet. And then he heard Jatayu's hoarse voice very close.

'Your chariot is going to burn up in no time, my friend,' Jatayu warned Dasharatha. 'I don't think it can carry you much longer.'

It was true—the clouds through which Dasharatha was riding were suddenly aflame too, and the heat was scorching and stifling.

'Come on, jump, get onto my back and I will fly you to Ayodhya,' offered Jatayu.

Dasharatha hesitated.

'Do not dither,' Jatayu said again. 'You must live to fight another day, if fight you must.' And so the king jumped, straight onto the mighty bird's back, a safe place to be. Jatayu's down of feathers was soft and comfortable—a secure refuge.

Shani was impressed by this show of courage and promised Dasharatha never to trouble him again. And on their return, Dasharatha and Jatayu were given a rapturous welcome in Ayodhya.

CHAPTER SIX

A PRINCE AND A DEMONESS IN LOVE

It was only a few years later, when Kaikeyi, who was Rama's stepmother, reminded Dasharatha of the promise he had made her when she had saved his life during battle. This was when a particularly fearsome demon Samparasura had attacked Heaven, and Dasharatha was called upon to join the army of Indra, the Lord of Heaven, to fight the demon. The confrontation raged on for days upon days, and in this battle too Jatayu had helped Dasharatha. Their friendship was further strengthened, as friendships often are when two friends fight together in the face of danger.

Kaikeyi, Dasharatha's favourite wife, had accompanied him. Suddenly, the axle of the wheel of Dasharatha's chariot broke. But Kaikeyi was alert and had reached out quickly to steady the wheel. Later, when Dasharatha fainted while fighting, she had driven the chariot away from the battlefield, saving his life. As a reward for Kaikeyi's presence of mind, Dasharatha had granted her

two boons and in return for one of them, she extracted a terrible price from him. Dasharatha was forced to send away his beloved eldest son Rama to the forest for fourteen years of exile, as Kaikeyi wanted her son Bharata to rule in his place.

Even though Bharata refused to sit on the throne, and only ruled on his brother's behalf, Rama the ever dutiful son, left for the forest in a hermit's robe. Accompanying him were his wife Sita and brother Lakshmana.

After staying at Chitrakoot near the river Mandakini for some time, the three reached the forests of Panchavati, where lived the ancient Jatayu, Rama's father's friend.

He flew down to meet the three of them and in a gentle speech, introduced himself. 'Son, I am a friend of your father's. I hope he is well.' He did not know that Dasharatha had died of grief within days of Rama's leaving Ayodhya. Rama had to break the sad news to Jatayu.

The king of birds bowed his great big head, beat his wings heavily on the rocks and lamented, 'How did you leave me, dear friend!' he sobbed, woebegone. 'Do you remember the way we fought together, standing shoulder to shoulder as we defeated Samparasura. After that battle, you had told me that we were such true friends that you were the body and I was your soul. How is it that the God of Death, Yama, took the body away to Heaven, when the soul still wanders the earth?' Jatayu wept, inconsolable.

His sadness moved Rama to tears as well. He embraced Jatayu respectfully. He knew about Jatayu's friendship with his father and the unwavering loyalty Jatayu had displayed on many occasions.

Jatayu wiped away his tears and told the three that he would protect them. 'I shall guard your dwelling, for this beautiful forest is frequented by greedy and evil beasts and ogres and *asuras* of all kinds. And dear son, when you go out hunting with Lakshmana, I shall watch over Sita.'

Rama, Lakshmana and Sita settled down in Panchavati. Unknown to them, they were being carefully watched by the *rakshasi* sister of Ravana, Surpanakha, who had noticed the three strangers and fallen in love with Rama. She hoped that he too would fall in love with her and marry her.

So one afternoon, as the three of them rested in the courtyard, Surpanakha approached them. She had changed her appearance, as *rakshasas* and *asuras* were able to do, and she now looked like a very beautiful girl, with a lovely smile. She made her way to Rama and blushingly told him, 'Handsome sage, I have fallen in love with you—please agree to make me your wife.'

Rama was amused. Pointing to Sita, he told her regretfully that he had vowed to marry only once, but there was his younger brother who had no such compulsions. No sooner had Surpanakha made her move towards Lakshmana than the angry younger brother maimed her with his sword.

Wounded, spurned and humiliated, Surpanakha assumed her terrible *rakshasi* self: eyes red and glaring, heavy locks of hair sprawled on her shoulders, and sharp, curved claws on her hands and feet. 'You have insulted me and my love,' she declared, sending shivers down Sita's spine, 'and I shall have my revenge.'

CHAPTER SEVEN

A KIDNAPPING IN THE FOREST

Ravana, when he heard of this incident, was angrier than Surpanakha could ever be. Not only had his sister been humiliated, but also those who had done this were the sons of his sworn enemy, Dasharatha. He reassured his sister, his evil mind already plotting revenge. 'Don't worry, sister,' he consoled her, 'we will make them pay for this.'

And so in days, a golden deer appeared at the gate of the trio's hermitage, and enticed Sita no end. It was

such an exquisite creature that Sita longed to have it for a pet and Rama, who did everything he could to please her, promised to go and get it for her.

However, Rama knew that Ravana would plan his revenge any moment. He wanted Sita to be safe and so he left Lakshmana behind at the hermitage to protect her from danger.

The deer was actually Ravana's uncle, Maricha, who had changed his form. Rama set off in pursuit of the golden deer and Maricha as the deer did not bother to hide himself because, of course, it was part of a trap. No sooner had Rama's arrows struck Maricha than the deer set up a piteous wail, calling out in Rama's voice, 'Help me, dear brother, help me.' Sita heard this far away and urged Lakshmana to set off, saying, 'Your brother's in danger. Go and help him.'

Lakshmana hesitated because his brother had asked him to stay with Sita no matter what happened. Seeing him hesitate, Sita scolded him for not caring enough for his brother and for not rushing to his help when he needed it.

Very reluctantly, Lakshmana left, but not before he had drawn a line around the hermitage, warning Sita that she mustn't step out beyond it, otherwise it could be very dangerous.

Yet no sooner had he left than Ravana, who had been keeping an eye on the whole situation, appeared, and he too had changed the way he looked. He stood at the gate of the hermitage as a holy man dressed in rags, begging for alms. Sita asked him to step in, but he wouldn't, and so she, unthinking of what was to follow, stepped across the line that Lakshmana had warned her not to cross—and straight away paid the price.

Ravana assumed his original *rakshasa* form, grabbed Sita and wouldn't let her go. She flailed against him, but he was stronger. Laughing demonically at her attempts to free herself, he rushed with her to his waiting flying chariot and took to the skies. He intended to reach his kingdom—Lanka—as soon as he possibly could.

CHAPTER EIGHT

A BATTLE UNTO DEATH

Old Jatayu had been half dozing on a tree. But the sound of Sita's wails woke him, and he was startled to see a chariot flying past. He made no mistake in recognizing Sita's cries and he also knew that it was Ravana who had kidnapped her and was taking her forcibly away to his kingdom.

Sita caught sight of him too, and pleaded with him to come to her help. She was no match for Ravana, for he was the strongest of all *rakshasa*s. There was only his

brother Kumbhakarana, who was far stronger, but then he slept most of the year.

Jatayu did not hesitate. He threw himself in the path of Ravana's chariot and tried to stop it advancing. Sita cried louder than before. 'You will not be able to stop this demon, Great Bird,' she said. 'You cannot stop the King of Lanka from taking me away. He is too strong for any of us. Fly to Rama and Lakshmana and tell them of my helpless plight!'

Jatayu knew he was much older and weaker, now with age upon him, and that Ravana was mighty and very powerful. But all he cared about was helping Sita, and he could not bear to see her distress. He thought of his friend Dasharatha, now no longer alive, and of his promise to Rama, and resolved that this outrage should not occur as long as he lived to prevent it.

Jatayu spoke to Ravana: 'O King of Rakshasas, I am Jatayu, King of Birds, and the mightiest of all winged creatures. Listen to me—let Sita go. A king's duty is to protect his subjects, and guard the honour of women, and here you are, kidnapping a woman and doing so in the most devious and cowardly way possible. Remember Sita is a princess, the wife of Rama, the Prince of Ayodhya. If you do not give her up, you will suffer the worst consequences possible. You are inviting death if you choose to carry out your evil intention of taking her away to Lanka.'

Ravana paid no heed to Jatayu's well-meant advice. Instead, he only threw back his head and roared with laughter. His cruel crowing rolled out across the skies and scattered the clouds.

Jatayu persisted. 'Apologize to Sita and return her to the hermitage. Once her husband Prince Rama returns, you will surely have to pay the price for this wickedness. You are only asking for punishment for your actions. Slowly, but surely, Yama, the God of Death, is tightening his noose around your neck. I am old and weaponless, and you are young, armed to the teeth and seated in a chariot that flies. But I will not look on helplessly if you do not stop now.'

Ravana flared up in a terrible rage. He attacked Jatayu with a sword, but at the beginning, they were evenly matched. The battle raged in the skies above the forest. Jatayu refused to give up, taking on Ravana with his giant claws and his mighty wings. He continued to berate Ravana, hoping the *rakshasa* would come to his senses and free Sita.

'Why did you commit this cowardly act when Rama and Lakshmana were away?' Jatayu continued. 'If you are indeed a brave king, fight Rama face to face. In any case, you shall not escape his wrath. I will not let you go, not till I am alive. I do not care for your fancy chariot or your multiple heads, or all the weapons you

possess! Fight me! Show me you are not a coward as well as a thief!'

Ravana kept aiming deadly arrows at him. But Jatayu faced these without flinching, and with his sharp talons, tore Ravana's flesh, making the blood run freely, angering Ravana even more. To think he was being stopped by an aged, stooping bird—so what if he called himself the king of the birds! Ravana furiously aimed sharp, serpentine missiles at Jatayu.

Jatayu was badly wounded, but he fought on, refusing to give up. His age was telling on him, but he kept on fighting valiantly, gathering up all his strength time and again to launch a fresh attack on Ravana. Ignoring his many wounds, he attacked Ravana fiercely and with his wings tore away Ravana's heavily jewelled crown, and also deprived him of his bow. Next, he stormed the chariot and killed the demon-faced mules and the charioteer, before smashing the vehicle into a thousand pieces. Ravana fell to the ground, still holding Sita. Those watching, even the gods in Heaven, cheered lustily as Ravana fell.

Now the old bird swooped down on Ravana's back and bit off great chunks of flesh from it. Next, he tried to tear away the arms that held onto Sita. But Ravana had her gripped tight and she remained helpless in his clutches.

When he knew that old Jatayu was not going to give up, Ravana let go of Sita for a moment. With a

brutal swipe of his sword, he swiftly cut off Jatayu's wings and talons. The old bird was too exhausted to stave off this attack. With his magnificent wings destroyed and his talons broken, Jatayu was now completely helpless. He fell to the ground, unable to move.

Sita looked at him in deep distress. 'O Great Bird! You fought so very bravely for me. You have been like a second father to my Lord, the Prince of Ayodhya, and now here you lie, injured and bleeding, and I cannot even help you.'

Ravana sheathed his sword, and seized Sita again. He assumed fearsome *rakshasa* proportions and flew into the sky with her. Caught in his grasp, Sita looked like a lightning flash across a huge black cloud coursing through the sky.

Jatayu lay in pain, waiting for Rama and Lakshmana. He knew they would come by in search of Sita, and he wanted to guide them in the right direction.

When they eventually did come that way, following the path indicated by the jewels Sita had dropped from the sky, they beheld a vulture huge as a mountain, writhing in agony. Suspecting him to be a *rakshasa*, Lakshmana rushed towards him, drawing his bow taut. The mighty vulture, however, addressing them both, said, 'I am the King of Birds, and a friend of your father Dasharatha.'

And then they saw that the creature was Jatayu, bereft of his once-mighty wings. Jatayu told them of his own defeat at the hands of Ravana. Rama then asked him where Ravana had taken Sita. Jatayu weakly pointed south with a nod of his head. As life ebbed away from his broken body, he lay with his head on Rama's lap and offered a prayer to him, for Rama was, after all, an incarnation of Vishnu:

'Be victorious, the bravest of all princes, the righteous one who will destroy Ravana! I bow to you, Rama, the ever merciful, who offers me hope of salvation so that I do not have to be reborn.'

Rama, with due respect for his father's friend, performed Jatayu's last rites as a son would. He understood that Jatayu wished to attain salvation, which could be achieved by visiting seven *tirtha*s or sacred places. Jatayu could not go to them, so Rama aimed an arrow deep into the ground to call up the holy rivers from all seven sacred places, so that Jatayu's wounded, scarred body could be cleansed and he could gain freedom from the endless cycle of births and deaths. Six rivers appeared one after the other instantly; Rama finally forced the seventh one to arrive at the spot.

As Jatayu was offered the waters of the seven *tirtha*s, he died peacefully, and became forever a symbol of courage and unstinting loyalty.

MythNotes

The place where Rama is thought to have found Jatayu is known as Jatayumangalam or Chadayamangalam in Kollam district in Kerala. There is a rock where Jatayu is thought to have fallen when he was fatally wounded by Ravana—and this is called Jatayupara. There is now a temple close to it, and nearby is a small pond shaped somewhat like a triangular beak.

People believe that when the injured Jatayu fell from the skies, his beak hit the rock, and caused a crater to be formed, from which water sprang. Jatayupara is the place where Rama first learned where Ravana had carried Sita, and Lakshmana spied some of the jewels that Sita had slipped off and thrown to mark the direction in which she was being forcibly taken. Legend goes that Rama gave the dying Jatayu water from this very pond before he could tell them what had happened.

Some people claim that the waters of the six rivers that Rama summoned are seen in one pond in Taaked village in Nashik in Maharashtra. The seventh lies a few feet away.